Dreamfarmer®'s Options Trading Journal

For Beginner Traders

To Eliminate FOMO One Trade at a Time

S. Rilynn Boyins

Dreamfarmer®'s

Options Trading Journal

Released September 2020

DISCLAIMER: I am in no way shape or form a financial professional. I am not authorized to provide any financial advice nor should you take any financial advice from me. This journal was created simply to help beginner Options Traders keep from FOMO and trade their plans as they build their own disciplines and strateigies.

Paperback ISBN: 978-1-7350161-2-2

How This Journal Works

This journal was designed for you to keep your emotions at bay and to stick to a trade plan. It is encouraged you do not hop into trades without doing your due diligence and having a plan.

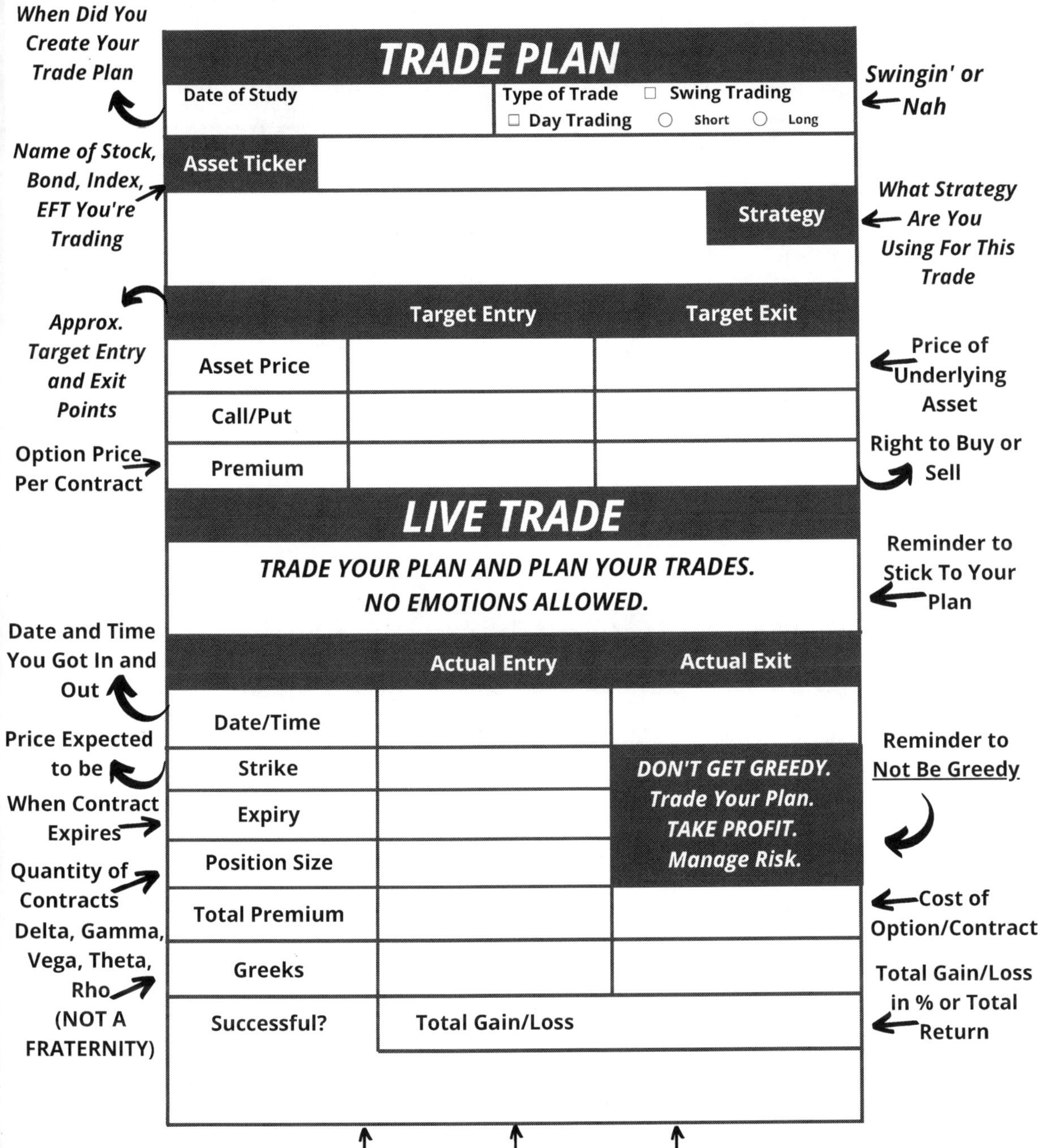

Did You follow your trade and gain/loss or did you not follow your trade and gain/loss? This section is important as it will help you learn from your trading mistakes, especially emotional ones. Feel free to add why you think it was or wasn't successful.

What is an Option?

The Right to Buy or Sell Something at a Specific Price

CALL= Right to Buy

If Price ↑ — Gain Profit $ $ $

If Price ↓ — Premium Paid is Loss $

PUT= Right to Sell

If Price ↑ — Premium Paid is Loss $

If Price ↓ — Gain Profit $ $ $

1 Contract = 100 Shares

Options Used On

What's The Trend?

Bullish ↑ — Price @ Support?
- ✔ YES — BUY
- ✖ NO — DON'T TRADE

Sideways — Wait For Breakout

Bearish ↓ — Price @ Resistance?
- ✔ YES — SELL
- ✖ NO — DON'T TRADE

Watch Lists

Trade What You See
Not What You Feel

Watch Lists

Trade What You See
Not What You Feel

Watch Lists

Trade What You See
Not What You Feel

THINGS TO NOTE

TRADE PLAN

Date of Study	Type of Trade ☐ Swing Trading ☐ Day Trading ○ Short ○ Long

Asset Ticker	

Strategy

	Target Entry	Target Exit
Asset Price		
Call/Put		
Premium		

LIVE TRADE

TRADE YOUR PLAN AND PLAN YOUR TRADES.
NO EMOTIONS ALLOWED.

	Actual Entry	Actual Exit
Date/Time		
Strike		***DON'T GET GREEDY. Trade Your Plan. TAKE PROFIT. Manage Risk.***
Expiry		
Position Size		
Total Premium		
Greeks		
Total Gain/Loss		

Successful?

THINGS TO NOTE

TRADE PLAN

Date of Study	Type of Trade ☐ Swing Trading ☐ Day Trading ◯ Short ◯ Long
Asset Ticker	
Strategy	

	Target Entry	Target Exit
Asset Price		
Call/Put		
Premium		

LIVE TRADE

TRADE YOUR PLAN AND PLAN YOUR TRADES.
NO EMOTIONS ALLOWED.

	Actual Entry	Actual Exit
Date/Time		
Strike		***DON'T GET GREEDY.*** *Trade Your Plan.* ***TAKE PROFIT.*** *Manage Risk.*
Expiry		
Position Size		
Total Premium		
Greeks		
Total Gain/Loss		
Successful?		

THINGS TO NOTE

TRADE PLAN

Date of Study	Type of Trade ☐ Swing Trading ☐ Day Trading ◯ Short ◯ Long

Asset Ticker	
Strategy	

	Target Entry	Target Exit
Asset Price		
Call/Put		
Premium		

LIVE TRADE

TRADE YOUR PLAN AND PLAN YOUR TRADES.
NO EMOTIONS ALLOWED.

	Actual Entry	Actual Exit
Date/Time		
Strike		***DON'T GET GREEDY. Trade Your Plan. TAKE PROFIT. Manage Risk.***
Expiry		
Position Size		
Total Premium		
Greeks		
Total Gain/Loss		

Successful?

THINGS TO NOTE

TRADE PLAN

Date of Study	Type of Trade ☐ Swing Trading ☐ Day Trading ○ Short ○ Long

Asset Ticker	

Strategy

	Target Entry	Target Exit
Asset Price		
Call/Put		
Premium		

LIVE TRADE

TRADE YOUR PLAN AND PLAN YOUR TRADES.
NO EMOTIONS ALLOWED.

	Actual Entry	Actual Exit
Date/Time		
Strike		***DON'T GET GREEDY. Trade Your Plan. TAKE PROFIT. Manage Risk.***
Expiry		
Position Size		
Total Premium		
Greeks		
Total Gain/Loss		

Successful?

THINGS TO NOTE

TRADE PLAN

Date of Study	Type of Trade ☐ Swing Trading ☐ Day Trading ◯ Short ◯ Long

Asset Ticker	
Strategy	

	Target Entry	Target Exit
Asset Price		
Call/Put		
Premium		

LIVE TRADE

TRADE YOUR PLAN AND PLAN YOUR TRADES.
NO EMOTIONS ALLOWED.

	Actual Entry	Actual Exit
Date/Time		
Strike		***DON'T GET GREEDY.*** *Trade Your Plan.* ***TAKE PROFIT.*** *Manage Risk.*
Expiry		
Position Size		
Total Premium		
Greeks		
Total Gain/Loss		
Successful?		

LESSONS LEARNED

This is a space to take note of any new indicators you've learned and lessons from mistakes you've made from these last 5 trades.

What is an Option?

The Right to Buy or Sell Something at a Specific Price

CALL= Right to Buy

If Price ↑ Gain Profit

If Price ↓ Premium Paid is Loss

PUT= Right to Sell

If Price ↑ Premium Paid is Loss

If Price ↓ Gain Profit

1 Contract = 100 Shares

Options Used On

What's The Trend?

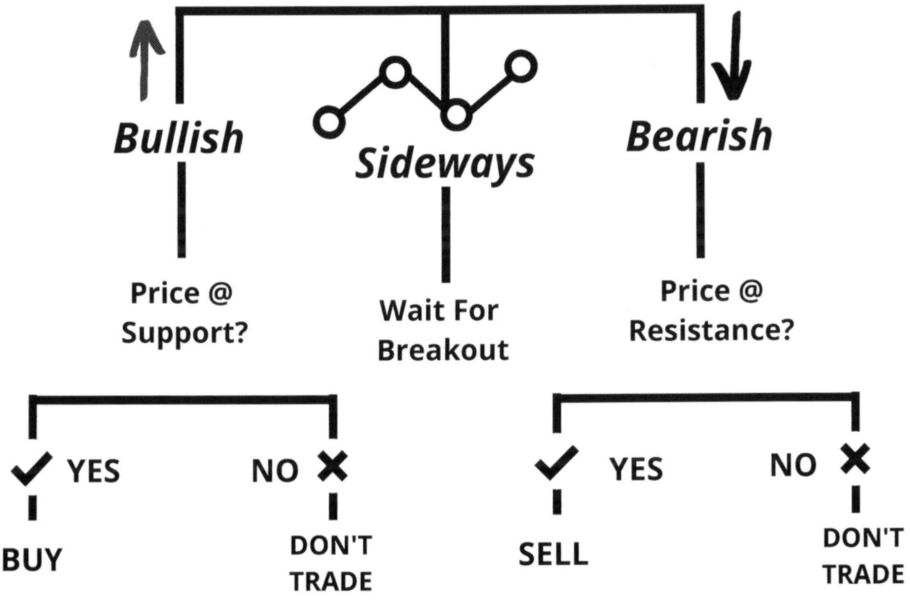

THINGS TO NOTE

TRADE PLAN

Date of Study	Type of Trade ☐ Swing Trading ☐ Day Trading ○ Short ○ Long
Asset Ticker	
Strategy	

	Target Entry	Target Exit
Asset Price		
Call/Put		
Premium		

LIVE TRADE

TRADE YOUR PLAN AND PLAN YOUR TRADES.
NO EMOTIONS ALLOWED.

	Actual Entry	Actual Exit
Date/Time		
Strike		***DON'T GET GREEDY. Trade Your Plan. TAKE PROFIT. Manage Risk.***
Expiry		
Position Size		
Total Premium		
Greeks		
Total Gain/Loss		
Successful?		

THINGS TO NOTE

TRADE PLAN

Date of Study	Type of Trade ☐ Swing Trading ☐ Day Trading ○ Short ○ Long

Asset Ticker	

Strategy

	Target Entry	Target Exit
Asset Price		
Call/Put		
Premium		

LIVE TRADE

TRADE YOUR PLAN AND PLAN YOUR TRADES.
NO EMOTIONS ALLOWED.

	Actual Entry	Actual Exit
Date/Time		
Strike		*DON'T GET GREEDY. Trade Your Plan. TAKE PROFIT. Manage Risk.*
Expiry		
Position Size		
Total Premium		
Greeks		
Total Gain/Loss		

Successful?

THINGS TO NOTE

TRADE PLAN

Date of Study	Type of Trade ☐ Swing Trading ☐ Day Trading ○ Short ○ Long
Asset Ticker	
Strategy	

	Target Entry	Target Exit
Asset Price		
Call/Put		
Premium		

LIVE TRADE

TRADE YOUR PLAN AND PLAN YOUR TRADES.
NO EMOTIONS ALLOWED.

	Actual Entry	Actual Exit
Date/Time		
Strike		***DON'T GET GREEDY.*** *Trade Your Plan.* ***TAKE PROFIT.*** *Manage Risk.*
Expiry		
Position Size		
Total Premium		
Greeks		
Total Gain/Loss		
Successful?		

THINGS TO NOTE

TRADE PLAN

Date of Study	Type of Trade ☐ Swing Trading ☐ Day Trading ○ Short ○ Long

Asset Ticker	
Strategy	

	Target Entry	Target Exit
Asset Price		
Call/Put		
Premium		

LIVE TRADE

TRADE YOUR PLAN AND PLAN YOUR TRADES.
NO EMOTIONS ALLOWED.

	Actual Entry	Actual Exit
Date/Time		
Strike		***DON'T GET GREEDY.*** *Trade Your Plan.* ***TAKE PROFIT.*** *Manage Risk.*
Expiry		
Position Size		
Total Premium		
Greeks		
Total Gain/Loss		

Successful?

THINGS TO NOTE

TRADE PLAN

Date of Study	Type of Trade ☐ Swing Trading ☐ Day Trading ◯ Short ◯ Long

Asset Ticker

Strategy

	Target Entry	Target Exit
Asset Price		
Call/Put		
Premium		

LIVE TRADE

TRADE YOUR PLAN AND PLAN YOUR TRADES.
NO EMOTIONS ALLOWED.

	Actual Entry	Actual Exit
Date/Time		
Strike		***DON'T GET GREEDY. Trade Your Plan. TAKE PROFIT. Manage Risk.***
Expiry		
Position Size		
Total Premium		
Greeks		
Total Gain/Loss		

Successful?

LESSONS LEARNED

This is a space to take note of any new indicators you've learned and lessons from mistakes you've made from these last 5 trades.

What is an Option?

The Right to Buy or Sell Something at a Specific Price

CALL= Right to Buy

If Price ↑ — Gain Profit $ $ $

If Price ↓ — Premium Paid is Loss $

PUT= Right to Sell

If Price ↑ — Premium Paid is Loss $

If Price ↓ — Gain Profit $ $ $

1 Contract = 100 Shares

Options Used On

What's The Trend?

Bullish — Price @ Support?
- YES → BUY
- NO → DON'T TRADE

Sideways — Wait For Breakout

Bearish — Price @ Resistance?
- YES → SELL
- NO → DON'T TRADE

THINGS TO NOTE

TRADE PLAN

Date of Study	Type of Trade ☐ Swing Trading ☐ Day Trading ◯ Short ◯ Long
Asset Ticker	
Strategy	

	Target Entry	Target Exit
Asset Price		
Call/Put		
Premium		

LIVE TRADE

TRADE YOUR PLAN AND PLAN YOUR TRADES.
NO EMOTIONS ALLOWED.

	Actual Entry	Actual Exit
Date/Time		
Strike		***DON'T GET GREEDY. Trade Your Plan. TAKE PROFIT. Manage Risk.***
Expiry		
Position Size		
Total Premium		
Greeks		
Total Gain/Loss		
Successful?		

THINGS TO NOTE

TRADE PLAN

Date of Study	Type of Trade ☐ Swing Trading ☐ Day Trading ○ Short ○ Long

Asset Ticker	

Strategy

	Target Entry	Target Exit
Asset Price		
Call/Put		
Premium		

LIVE TRADE

TRADE YOUR PLAN AND PLAN YOUR TRADES.
NO EMOTIONS ALLOWED.

	Actual Entry	Actual Exit
Date/Time		
Strike		***DON'T GET GREEDY. Trade Your Plan. TAKE PROFIT. Manage Risk.***
Expiry		
Position Size		
Total Premium		
Greeks		
Total Gain/Loss		

Successful?

THINGS TO NOTE

TRADE PLAN

Date of Study	Type of Trade ☐ Swing Trading ☐ Day Trading ○ Short ○ Long

Asset Ticker	
Strategy	

	Target Entry	Target Exit
Asset Price		
Call/Put		
Premium		

LIVE TRADE

TRADE YOUR PLAN AND PLAN YOUR TRADES.
NO EMOTIONS ALLOWED.

	Actual Entry	Actual Exit
Date/Time		
Strike		***DON'T GET GREEDY. Trade Your Plan. TAKE PROFIT. Manage Risk.***
Expiry		
Position Size		
Total Premium		
Greeks		
Total Gain/Loss		
Successful?		

THINGS TO NOTE

TRADE PLAN

Date of Study	Type of Trade ☐ Swing Trading ☐ Day Trading ◯ Short ◯ Long
Asset Ticker	
Strategy	

	Target Entry	Target Exit
Asset Price		
Call/Put		
Premium		

LIVE TRADE

TRADE YOUR PLAN AND PLAN YOUR TRADES.
NO EMOTIONS ALLOWED.

	Actual Entry	Actual Exit
Date/Time		
Strike		***DON'T GET GREEDY. Trade Your Plan. TAKE PROFIT. Manage Risk.***
Expiry		
Position Size		
Total Premium		
Greeks		
Total Gain/Loss		
Successful?		

THINGS TO NOTE

TRADE PLAN

Date of Study	Type of Trade ☐ Swing Trading ☐ Day Trading ◯ Short ◯ Long

Asset Ticker	

Strategy

	Target Entry	Target Exit
Asset Price		
Call/Put		
Premium		

LIVE TRADE

TRADE YOUR PLAN AND PLAN YOUR TRADES.
NO EMOTIONS ALLOWED.

	Actual Entry	Actual Exit
Date/Time		
Strike		***DON'T GET GREEDY.*** ***Trade Your Plan.*** ***TAKE PROFIT.*** ***Manage Risk.***
Expiry		
Position Size		
Total Premium		
Greeks		
Total Gain/Loss		

Successful?

LESSONS LEARNED

This is a space to take note of any new indicators you've learned and lessons from mistakes you've made from these last 5 trades.

What is an Option?

The Right to Buy or Sell Something at a Specific Price

CALL= Right to Buy

If Price ↑ — Gain Profit $ $ $

If Price ↓ — Premium Paid is Loss $

PUT= Right to Sell

If Price ↑ — Premium Paid is Loss $

If Price ↓ — Gain Profit $ $ $

1 Contract = 100 Shares

Options Used On

What's The Trend?

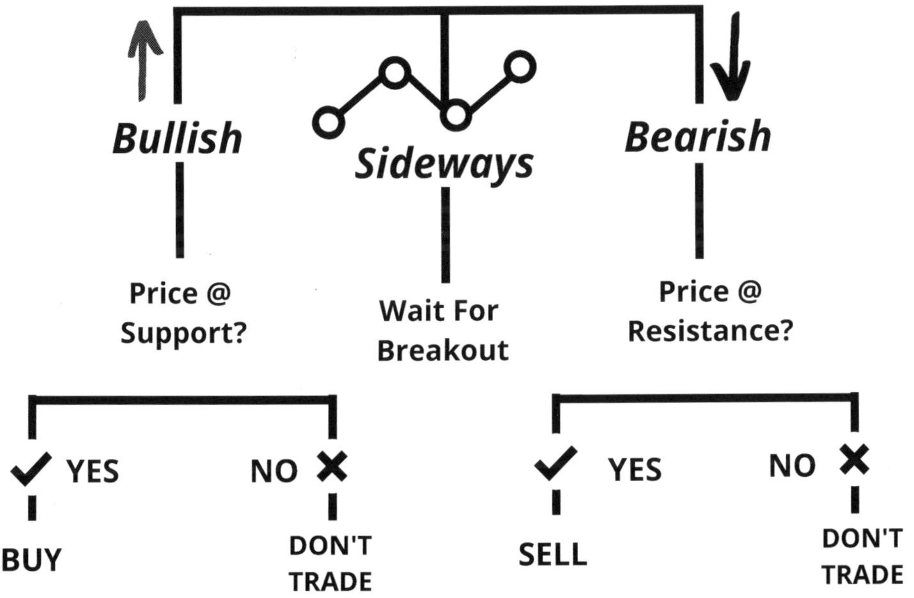

THINGS TO NOTE

TRADE PLAN

Date of Study	Type of Trade ☐ Swing Trading ☐ Day Trading ◯ Short ◯ Long

Asset Ticker	
Strategy	

	Target Entry	Target Exit
Asset Price		
Call/Put		
Premium		

LIVE TRADE

TRADE YOUR PLAN AND PLAN YOUR TRADES.
NO EMOTIONS ALLOWED.

	Actual Entry	Actual Exit
Date/Time		
Strike		***DON'T GET GREEDY. Trade Your Plan. TAKE PROFIT. Manage Risk.***
Expiry		
Position Size		
Total Premium		
Greeks		
Total Gain/Loss		
Successful?		

THINGS TO NOTE

TRADE PLAN

Date of Study	Type of Trade ☐ Swing Trading ☐ Day Trading ○ Short ○ Long

Asset Ticker	

Strategy

	Target Entry	Target Exit
Asset Price		
Call/Put		
Premium		

LIVE TRADE

TRADE YOUR PLAN AND PLAN YOUR TRADES.
NO EMOTIONS ALLOWED.

	Actual Entry	Actual Exit
Date/Time		
Strike		***DON'T GET GREEDY.*** *Trade Your Plan.* ***TAKE PROFIT.*** *Manage Risk.*
Expiry		
Position Size		
Total Premium		
Greeks		
Total Gain/Loss		

Successful?

THINGS TO NOTE

TRADE PLAN

Date of Study	Type of Trade ☐ Swing Trading ☐ Day Trading ◯ Short ◯ Long

Asset Ticker	

Strategy

	Target Entry	Target Exit
Asset Price		
Call/Put		
Premium		

LIVE TRADE

TRADE YOUR PLAN AND PLAN YOUR TRADES.
NO EMOTIONS ALLOWED.

	Actual Entry	Actual Exit
Date/Time		
Strike		***DON'T GET GREEDY.*** *Trade Your Plan.* ***TAKE PROFIT.*** *Manage Risk.*
Expiry		
Position Size		
Total Premium		
Greeks		
Total Gain/Loss		

Successful?

THINGS TO NOTE

TRADE PLAN

Date of Study	Type of Trade ☐ Swing Trading ☐ Day Trading ○ Short ○ Long
Asset Ticker	
Strategy	

	Target Entry	Target Exit
Asset Price		
Call/Put		
Premium		

LIVE TRADE

TRADE YOUR PLAN AND PLAN YOUR TRADES.
NO EMOTIONS ALLOWED.

	Actual Entry	Actual Exit
Date/Time		
Strike		*DON'T GET GREEDY. Trade Your Plan. TAKE PROFIT. Manage Risk.*
Expiry		
Position Size		
Total Premium		
Greeks		
Total Gain/Loss		
Successful?		

THINGS TO NOTE

TRADE PLAN

Date of Study	Type of Trade ☐ Swing Trading ☐ Day Trading ◯ Short ◯ Long
Asset Ticker	
Strategy	

	Target Entry	Target Exit
Asset Price		
Call/Put		
Premium		

LIVE TRADE

TRADE YOUR PLAN AND PLAN YOUR TRADES.
NO EMOTIONS ALLOWED.

	Actual Entry	Actual Exit
Date/Time		
Strike		***DON'T GET GREEDY. Trade Your Plan. TAKE PROFIT. Manage Risk.***
Expiry		
Position Size		
Total Premium		
Greeks		
Total Gain/Loss		
Successful?		

LESSONS LEARNED

This is a space to take note of any new indicators you've learned and lessons from mistakes you've made from these last 5 trades.

What is an Option?

The Right to Buy or Sell Something at a Specific Price

CALL= Right to Buy

If Price ↑ Gain Profit $ $ $

If Price ↓ Premium Paid is Loss $

PUT= Right to Sell

If Price ↑ Premium Paid is Loss $

If Price ↓ Gain Profit $ $ $

1 Contract = 100 Shares

Options Used On

What's The Trend?

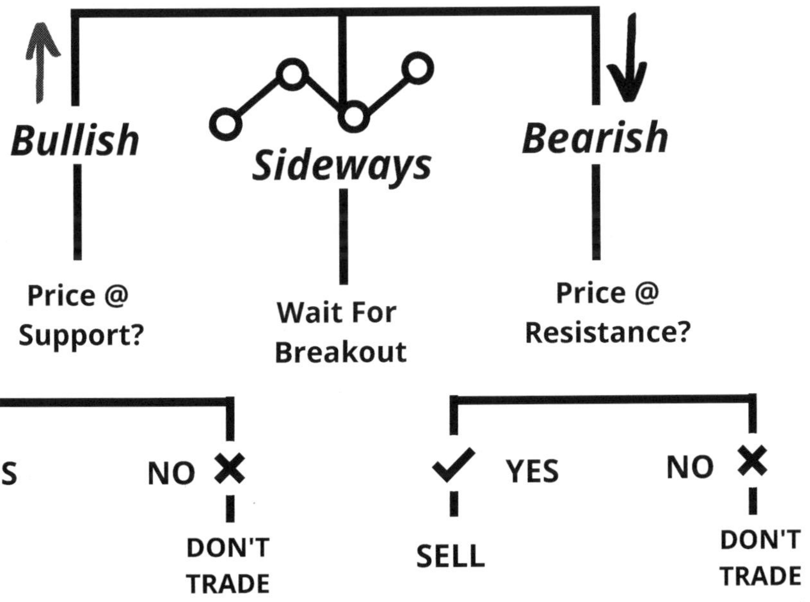

THINGS TO NOTE

TRADE PLAN

Date of Study	Type of Trade ☐ Swing Trading ☐ Day Trading ◯ Short ◯ Long

Asset Ticker	

Strategy

	Target Entry	Target Exit
Asset Price		
Call/Put		
Premium		

LIVE TRADE

TRADE YOUR PLAN AND PLAN YOUR TRADES.
NO EMOTIONS ALLOWED.

	Actual Entry	Actual Exit
Date/Time		
Strike		***DON'T GET GREEDY.***
Expiry		***Trade Your Plan.***
Position Size		***TAKE PROFIT. Manage Risk.***
Total Premium		
Greeks		
Total Gain/Loss		

Successful?

THINGS TO NOTE

TRADE PLAN

Date of Study	Type of Trade ☐ Swing Trading ☐ Day Trading ◯ Short ◯ Long
Asset Ticker	
Strategy	

	Target Entry	Target Exit
Asset Price		
Call/Put		
Premium		

LIVE TRADE

TRADE YOUR PLAN AND PLAN YOUR TRADES.
NO EMOTIONS ALLOWED.

	Actual Entry	Actual Exit
Date/Time		
Strike		***DON'T GET GREEDY. Trade Your Plan. TAKE PROFIT. Manage Risk.***
Expiry		
Position Size		
Total Premium		
Greeks		
Total Gain/Loss		

Successful?

THINGS TO NOTE

TRADE PLAN

Date of Study	Type of Trade ☐ Swing Trading ☐ Day Trading ○ Short ○ Long
Asset Ticker	
Strategy	

	Target Entry	Target Exit
Asset Price		
Call/Put		
Premium		

LIVE TRADE

TRADE YOUR PLAN AND PLAN YOUR TRADES.
NO EMOTIONS ALLOWED.

	Actual Entry	Actual Exit
Date/Time		
Strike		***DON'T GET GREEDY. Trade Your Plan. TAKE PROFIT. Manage Risk.***
Expiry		
Position Size		
Total Premium		
Greeks		
Total Gain/Loss		
Successful?		

THINGS TO NOTE

TRADE PLAN

Date of Study	Type of Trade ☐ Swing Trading ☐ Day Trading ◯ Short ◯ Long

Asset Ticker	
Strategy	

	Target Entry	Target Exit
Asset Price		
Call/Put		
Premium		

LIVE TRADE

TRADE YOUR PLAN AND PLAN YOUR TRADES.
NO EMOTIONS ALLOWED.

	Actual Entry	Actual Exit
Date/Time		
Strike		***DON'T GET GREEDY. Trade Your Plan. TAKE PROFIT. Manage Risk.***
Expiry		
Position Size		
Total Premium		
Greeks		
Total Gain/Loss		

Successful?

THINGS TO NOTE

TRADE PLAN

Date of Study	Type of Trade ☐ Swing Trading ☐ Day Trading ○ Short ○ Long

Asset Ticker	

Strategy

	Target Entry	Target Exit
Asset Price		
Call/Put		
Premium		

LIVE TRADE

TRADE YOUR PLAN AND PLAN YOUR TRADES.
NO EMOTIONS ALLOWED.

	Actual Entry	Actual Exit
Date/Time		
Strike		***DON'T GET GREEDY.***
Expiry		***Trade Your Plan.***
Position Size		***TAKE PROFIT. Manage Risk.***
Total Premium		
Greeks		
Total Gain/Loss		

Successful?

LESSONS LEARNED

This is a space to take note of any new indicators you've learned and lessons from mistakes you've made from these last 5 trades.

What is an Option?

The Right to Buy or Sell Something at a Specific Price

CALL= Right to Buy

If Price ↑ Gain Profit

If Price ↓ Premium Paid is Loss

PUT= Right to Sell

If Price ↑ Premium Paid is Loss

If Price ↓ Gain Profit

1 Contract = 100 Shares

Options Used On

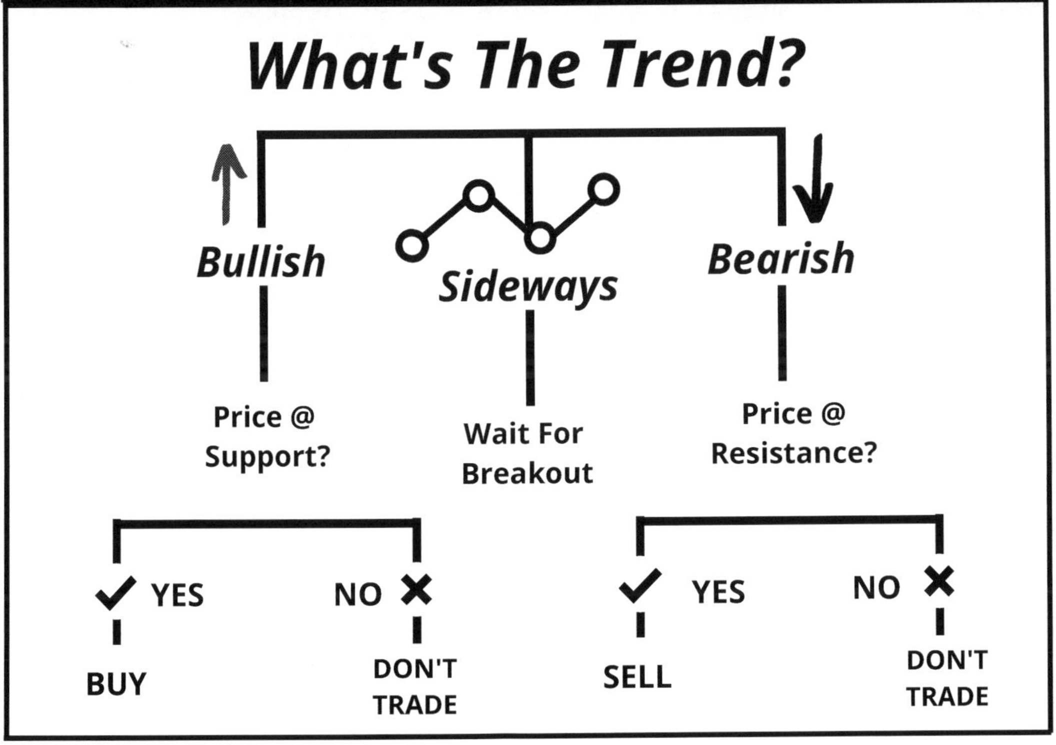

THINGS TO NOTE

TRADE PLAN

Date of Study	Type of Trade ☐ Swing Trading ☐ Day Trading ◯ Short ◯ Long

Asset Ticker	
Strategy	

	Target Entry	Target Exit
Asset Price		
Call/Put		
Premium		

LIVE TRADE

TRADE YOUR PLAN AND PLAN YOUR TRADES.
NO EMOTIONS ALLOWED.

	Actual Entry	Actual Exit
Date/Time		
Strike		***DON'T GET GREEDY. Trade Your Plan. TAKE PROFIT. Manage Risk.***
Expiry		
Position Size		
Total Premium		
Greeks		
Total Gain/Loss		
Successful?		

THINGS TO NOTE

TRADE PLAN

Date of Study	Type of Trade ☐ Swing Trading ☐ Day Trading ◯ Short ◯ Long
Asset Ticker	
Strategy	

	Target Entry	Target Exit
Asset Price		
Call/Put		
Premium		

LIVE TRADE

TRADE YOUR PLAN AND PLAN YOUR TRADES.
NO EMOTIONS ALLOWED.

	Actual Entry	Actual Exit
Date/Time		
Strike		***DON'T GET GREEDY. Trade Your Plan. TAKE PROFIT. Manage Risk.***
Expiry		
Position Size		
Total Premium		
Greeks		
Total Gain/Loss		
Successful?		

THINGS TO NOTE

TRADE PLAN

Date of Study	Type of Trade ☐ Swing Trading ☐ Day Trading ◯ Short ◯ Long

Asset Ticker	

Strategy

	Target Entry	Target Exit
Asset Price		
Call/Put		
Premium		

LIVE TRADE

TRADE YOUR PLAN AND PLAN YOUR TRADES.
NO EMOTIONS ALLOWED.

	Actual Entry	Actual Exit
Date/Time		
Strike		***DON'T GET GREEDY.*** *Trade Your Plan.* ***TAKE PROFIT.*** *Manage Risk.*
Expiry		
Position Size		
Total Premium		
Greeks		
Total Gain/Loss		

Successful?

THINGS TO NOTE

TRADE PLAN

Date of Study	**Type of Trade** ☐ Swing Trading ☐ Day Trading ◯ Short ◯ Long
Asset Ticker	
Strategy	

	Target Entry	Target Exit
Asset Price		
Call/Put		
Premium		

LIVE TRADE

TRADE YOUR PLAN AND PLAN YOUR TRADES. NO EMOTIONS ALLOWED.

	Actual Entry	Actual Exit
Date/Time		
Strike		***DON'T GET GREEDY. Trade Your Plan. TAKE PROFIT. Manage Risk.***
Expiry		
Position Size		
Total Premium		
Greeks		
Total Gain/Loss		

Successful?

THINGS TO NOTE

TRADE PLAN

Date of Study	Type of Trade ☐ Swing Trading ☐ Day Trading ○ Short ○ Long

Asset Ticker	

Strategy

	Target Entry	Target Exit
Asset Price		
Call/Put		
Premium		

LIVE TRADE

TRADE YOUR PLAN AND PLAN YOUR TRADES.
NO EMOTIONS ALLOWED.

	Actual Entry	Actual Exit
Date/Time		
Strike		***DON'T GET GREEDY.***
Expiry		***Trade Your Plan.***
Position Size		***TAKE PROFIT. Manage Risk.***
Total Premium		
Greeks		
Total Gain/Loss		

Successful?

LESSONS LEARNED

This is a space to take note of any new indicators you've learned and lessons from mistakes you've made from these last 5 trades.

What is an Option?

The Right to Buy or Sell Something at a Specific Price

CALL= Right to Buy

If Price ↑ — Gain Profit $ $ $

If Price ↓ — Premium Paid is Loss $

PUT= Right to Sell

If Price ↑ — Premium Paid is Loss $

If Price ↓ — Gain Profit $ $ $

1 Contract = 100 Shares

Options Used On

What's The Trend?

Bullish ↑ — Price @ Support?
- ✔ YES — BUY
- ✖ NO — DON'T TRADE

Sideways — Wait For Breakout

Bearish ↓ — Price @ Resistance?
- ✔ YES — SELL
- ✖ NO — DON'T TRADE

THINGS TO NOTE

TRADE PLAN

Date of Study	Type of Trade ☐ Swing Trading ☐ Day Trading ○ Short ○ Long

Asset Ticker

Strategy

	Target Entry	Target Exit
Asset Price		
Call/Put		
Premium		

LIVE TRADE

TRADE YOUR PLAN AND PLAN YOUR TRADES.
NO EMOTIONS ALLOWED.

	Actual Entry	Actual Exit
Date/Time		
Strike		***DON'T GET GREEDY. Trade Your Plan. TAKE PROFIT. Manage Risk.***
Expiry		
Position Size		
Total Premium		
Greeks		
Total Gain/Loss		

Successful?

THINGS TO NOTE

TRADE PLAN

Date of Study	Type of Trade ☐ Swing Trading ☐ Day Trading ◯ Short ◯ Long

Asset Ticker	

Strategy

	Target Entry	Target Exit
Asset Price		
Call/Put		
Premium		

LIVE TRADE

TRADE YOUR PLAN AND PLAN YOUR TRADES.
NO EMOTIONS ALLOWED.

	Actual Entry	Actual Exit
Date/Time		
Strike		***DON'T GET GREEDY. Trade Your Plan. TAKE PROFIT. Manage Risk.***
Expiry		
Position Size		
Total Premium		
Greeks		
Total Gain/Loss		

Successful?

THINGS TO NOTE

TRADE PLAN

Date of Study	Type of Trade ☐ Swing Trading ☐ Day Trading ◯ Short ◯ Long

Asset Ticker	
Strategy	

	Target Entry	Target Exit
Asset Price		
Call/Put		
Premium		

LIVE TRADE

TRADE YOUR PLAN AND PLAN YOUR TRADES.
NO EMOTIONS ALLOWED.

	Actual Entry	Actual Exit
Date/Time		
Strike		***DON'T GET GREEDY.***
Expiry		***Trade Your Plan.***
Position Size		***TAKE PROFIT. Manage Risk.***
Total Premium		
Greeks		
Total Gain/Loss		

Successful?

THINGS TO NOTE

TRADE PLAN

Date of Study	Type of Trade ☐ Swing Trading ☐ Day Trading ◯ Short ◯ Long
Asset Ticker	
Strategy	

	Target Entry	Target Exit
Asset Price		
Call/Put		
Premium		

LIVE TRADE

TRADE YOUR PLAN AND PLAN YOUR TRADES.
NO EMOTIONS ALLOWED.

	Actual Entry	Actual Exit
Date/Time		
Strike		***DON'T GET GREEDY.*** ***Trade Your Plan.*** ***TAKE PROFIT.*** ***Manage Risk.***
Expiry		
Position Size		
Total Premium		
Greeks		
Total Gain/Loss		
Successful?		

THINGS TO NOTE

TRADE PLAN

Date of Study

Type of Trade ☐ **Swing Trading** ☐ **Day Trading** ○ **Short** ○ **Long**

Asset Ticker

Strategy

	Target Entry	Target Exit
Asset Price		
Call/Put		
Premium		

LIVE TRADE

TRADE YOUR PLAN AND PLAN YOUR TRADES.
NO EMOTIONS ALLOWED.

	Actual Entry	Actual Exit
Date/Time		
Strike		***DON'T GET GREEDY. Trade Your Plan. TAKE PROFIT. Manage Risk.***
Expiry		
Position Size		
Total Premium		
Greeks		
Total Gain/Loss		

Successful?

LESSONS LEARNED

This is a space to take note of any new indicators you've learned and lessons from mistakes you've made from these last 5 trades.

What is an Option?

The Right to Buy or Sell Something at a Specific Price

CALL= Right to Buy

If Price ↑ — Gain Profit $ $ $

If Price ↓ — Premium Paid is Loss $

PUT= Right to Sell

If Price ↑ — Premium Paid is Loss $

If Price ↓ — Gain Profit $ $ $

1 Contract = 100 Shares

Options Used On

What's The Trend?

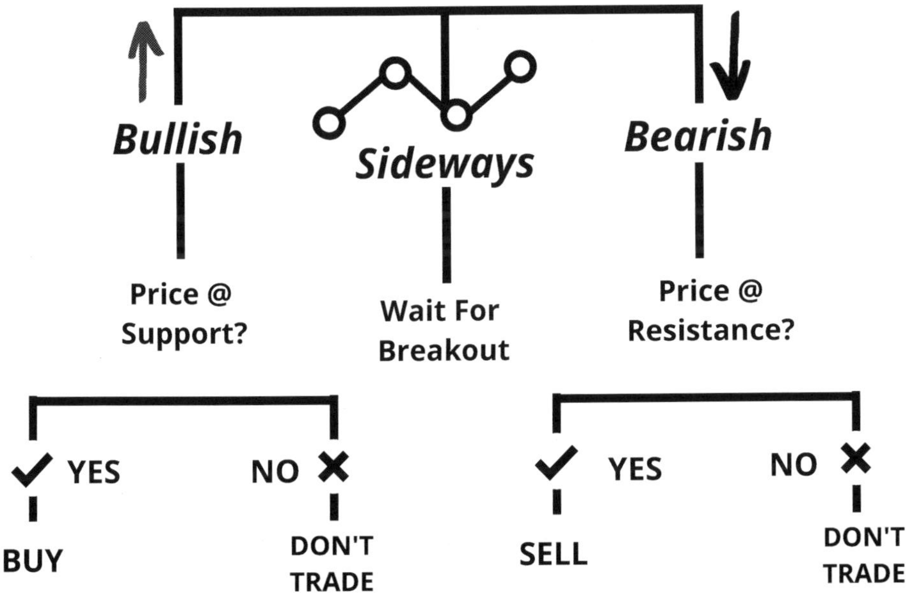

THINGS TO NOTE

TRADE PLAN

Date of Study	Type of Trade ☐ Swing Trading ☐ Day Trading ◯ Short ◯ Long
Asset Ticker	
Strategy	

	Target Entry	Target Exit
Asset Price		
Call/Put		
Premium		

LIVE TRADE

TRADE YOUR PLAN AND PLAN YOUR TRADES.
NO EMOTIONS ALLOWED.

	Actual Entry	Actual Exit
Date/Time		
Strike		***DON'T GET GREEDY. Trade Your Plan. TAKE PROFIT. Manage Risk.***
Expiry		
Position Size		
Total Premium		
Greeks		
Total Gain/Loss		
Successful?		

THINGS TO NOTE

TRADE PLAN

Date of Study	Type of Trade ☐ Swing Trading ☐ Day Trading ◯ Short ◯ Long

Asset Ticker	

Strategy

	Target Entry	Target Exit
Asset Price		
Call/Put		
Premium		

LIVE TRADE

TRADE YOUR PLAN AND PLAN YOUR TRADES.
NO EMOTIONS ALLOWED.

	Actual Entry	Actual Exit
Date/Time		
Strike		***DON'T GET GREEDY.*** *Trade Your Plan.* ***TAKE PROFIT.*** *Manage Risk.*
Expiry		
Position Size		
Total Premium		
Greeks		
Total Gain/Loss		

Successful?

THINGS TO NOTE

TRADE PLAN

Date of Study	Type of Trade ☐ Swing Trading ☐ Day Trading ◯ Short ◯ Long

Asset Ticker	

Strategy

	Target Entry	Target Exit
Asset Price		
Call/Put		
Premium		

LIVE TRADE

TRADE YOUR PLAN AND PLAN YOUR TRADES.
NO EMOTIONS ALLOWED.

	Actual Entry	Actual Exit
Date/Time		
Strike		***DON'T GET GREEDY.*** ***Trade Your Plan.*** ***TAKE PROFIT.*** ***Manage Risk.***
Expiry		
Position Size		
Total Premium		
Greeks		
Total Gain/Loss		

Successful?

THINGS TO NOTE

TRADE PLAN

Date of Study	**Type of Trade** ☐ Swing Trading ☐ Day Trading ◯ Short ◯ Long
Asset Ticker	
Strategy	

	Target Entry	Target Exit
Asset Price		
Call/Put		
Premium		

LIVE TRADE

TRADE YOUR PLAN AND PLAN YOUR TRADES.
NO EMOTIONS ALLOWED.

	Actual Entry	Actual Exit
Date/Time		
Strike		***DON'T GET GREEDY. Trade Your Plan. TAKE PROFIT. Manage Risk.***
Expiry		
Position Size		
Total Premium		
Greeks		
Total Gain/Loss		
Successful?		

THINGS TO NOTE

TRADE PLAN

Date of Study	Type of Trade ☐ Swing Trading ☐ Day Trading ◯ Short ◯ Long

Asset Ticker

Strategy

	Target Entry	Target Exit
Asset Price		
Call/Put		
Premium		

LIVE TRADE

TRADE YOUR PLAN AND PLAN YOUR TRADES. NO EMOTIONS ALLOWED.

	Actual Entry	Actual Exit
Date/Time		
Strike		*DON'T GET GREEDY. Trade Your Plan. TAKE PROFIT. Manage Risk.*
Expiry		
Position Size		
Total Premium		
Greeks		
Total Gain/Loss		

Successful?

LESSONS LEARNED

This is a space to take note of any new indicators you've learned and lessons from mistakes you've made from these last 5 trades.

What is an Option?

The Right to Buy or Sell Something at a Specific Price

CALL= Right to Buy

If Price ↑ Gain Profit $ $ $

If Price ↓ Premium Paid is Loss $

PUT= Right to Sell

If Price ↑ Premium Paid is Loss $

If Price ↓ Gain Profit $ $ $

1 Contract = 100 Shares

Options Used On

What's The Trend?

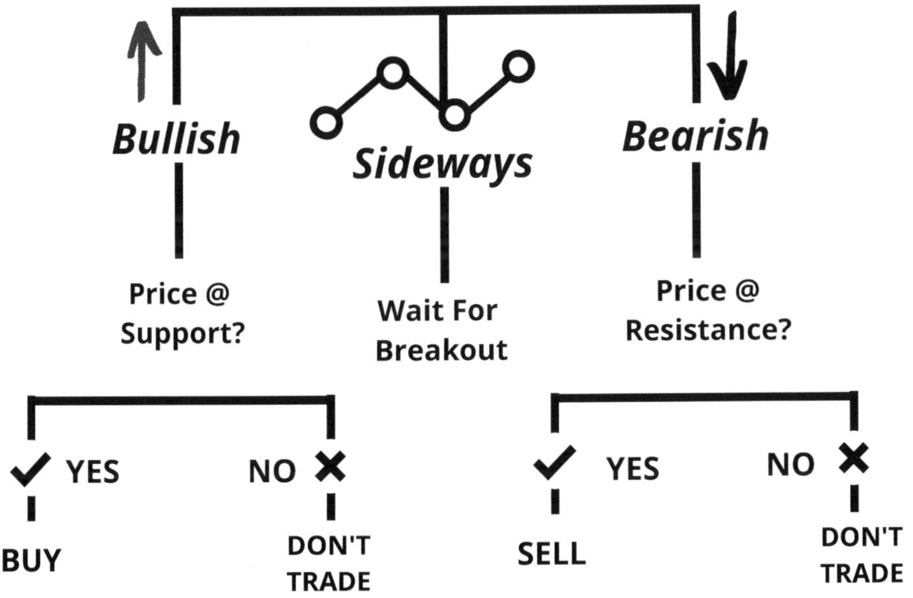

THINGS TO NOTE

TRADE PLAN

Date of Study	Type of Trade ☐ Swing Trading ☐ Day Trading ◯ Short ◯ Long
Asset Ticker	
Strategy	

	Target Entry	Target Exit
Asset Price		
Call/Put		
Premium		

LIVE TRADE

TRADE YOUR PLAN AND PLAN YOUR TRADES.
NO EMOTIONS ALLOWED.

	Actual Entry	Actual Exit
Date/Time		
Strike		***DON'T GET GREEDY. Trade Your Plan. TAKE PROFIT. Manage Risk.***
Expiry		
Position Size		
Total Premium		
Greeks		
Total Gain/Loss		
Successful?		

THINGS TO NOTE

Beginner and Advanced Options Trading Courses at Dreamfarmer.org

TRADE PLAN

Date of Study	Type of Trade ☐ Swing Trading ☐ Day Trading ◯ Short ◯ Long

Asset Ticker	

Strategy

	Target Entry	Target Exit
Asset Price		
Call/Put		
Premium		

LIVE TRADE

TRADE YOUR PLAN AND PLAN YOUR TRADES.
NO EMOTIONS ALLOWED.

	Actual Entry	Actual Exit
Date/Time		
Strike		***DON'T GET GREEDY.***
Expiry		***Trade Your Plan.***
Position Size		***TAKE PROFIT. Manage Risk.***
Total Premium		
Greeks		
Total Gain/Loss		

Successful?

THINGS TO NOTE

TRADE PLAN

Date of Study	Type of Trade ☐ Swing Trading ☐ Day Trading ◯ Short ◯ Long

Asset Ticker	

Strategy

	Target Entry	Target Exit
Asset Price		
Call/Put		
Premium		

LIVE TRADE

TRADE YOUR PLAN AND PLAN YOUR TRADES.
NO EMOTIONS ALLOWED.

	Actual Entry	Actual Exit
Date/Time		
Strike		***DON'T GET GREEDY. Trade Your Plan. TAKE PROFIT. Manage Risk.***
Expiry		
Position Size		
Total Premium		
Greeks		
Total Gain/Loss		

Successful?

THINGS TO NOTE

TRADE PLAN

Date of Study	**Type of Trade** ☐ **Swing Trading** ☐ **Day Trading** ○ **Short** ○ **Long**
Asset Ticker	
Strategy	

	Target Entry	Target Exit
Asset Price		
Call/Put		
Premium		

LIVE TRADE

TRADE YOUR PLAN AND PLAN YOUR TRADES.
NO EMOTIONS ALLOWED.

	Actual Entry	Actual Exit
Date/Time		
Strike		***DON'T GET GREEDY. Trade Your Plan. TAKE PROFIT. Manage Risk.***
Expiry		
Position Size		
Total Premium		
Greeks		
Total Gain/Loss		
Successful?		

THINGS TO NOTE

TRADE PLAN

Date of Study	Type of Trade ☐ Swing Trading ☐ Day Trading ◯ Short ◯ Long

Asset Ticker	

Strategy

	Target Entry	Target Exit
Asset Price		
Call/Put		
Premium		

LIVE TRADE

TRADE YOUR PLAN AND PLAN YOUR TRADES.
NO EMOTIONS ALLOWED.

	Actual Entry	Actual Exit
Date/Time		
Strike		***DON'T GET GREEDY. Trade Your Plan. TAKE PROFIT. Manage Risk.***
Expiry		
Position Size		
Total Premium		
Greeks		
Total Gain/Loss		

Successful?

LESSONS LEARNED

This is a space to take note of any new indicators you've learned and lessons from mistakes you've made from these last 5 trades.

What is an Option?

The Right to Buy or Sell Something at a Specific Price

CALL= Right to Buy

If Price ↑ — Gain Profit $ $ $

If Price ↓ — Premium Paid is Loss $

PUT= Right to Sell

If Price ↑ — Premium Paid is Loss $

If Price ↓ — Gain Profit $ $ $

1 Contract = 100 Shares

Options Used On

What's The Trend?

Bullish ↑ — Price @ Support?
- ✔ YES — BUY
- ✖ NO — DON'T TRADE

Sideways — Wait For Breakout

Bearish ↓ — Price @ Resistance?
- ✔ YES — SELL
- ✖ NO — DON'T TRADE

THINGS TO NOTE

TRADE PLAN

Date of Study	Type of Trade ☐ Swing Trading ☐ Day Trading ○ Short ○ Long

Asset Ticker	
Strategy	

	Target Entry	Target Exit
Asset Price		
Call/Put		
Premium		

LIVE TRADE

TRADE YOUR PLAN AND PLAN YOUR TRADES.
NO EMOTIONS ALLOWED.

	Actual Entry	Actual Exit
Date/Time		
Strike		***DON'T GET GREEDY.***
Expiry		***Trade Your Plan.***
Position Size		***TAKE PROFIT.*** ***Manage Risk.***
Total Premium		
Greeks		
Total Gain/Loss		
Successful?		

THINGS TO NOTE

TRADE PLAN

Date of Study	Type of Trade ☐ Swing Trading ☐ Day Trading ◯ Short ◯ Long

Asset Ticker	
Strategy	

	Target Entry	Target Exit
Asset Price		
Call/Put		
Premium		

LIVE TRADE

TRADE YOUR PLAN AND PLAN YOUR TRADES.
NO EMOTIONS ALLOWED.

	Actual Entry	Actual Exit
Date/Time		
Strike		***DON'T GET GREEDY. Trade Your Plan. TAKE PROFIT. Manage Risk.***
Expiry		
Position Size		
Total Premium		
Greeks		
Total Gain/Loss		
Successful?		

THINGS TO NOTE

TRADE PLAN

Date of Study	Type of Trade ☐ Swing Trading ☐ Day Trading ◯ Short ◯ Long
Asset Ticker	
Strategy	

	Target Entry	Target Exit
Asset Price		
Call/Put		
Premium		

LIVE TRADE

TRADE YOUR PLAN AND PLAN YOUR TRADES.
NO EMOTIONS ALLOWED.

	Actual Entry	Actual Exit
Date/Time		
Strike		***DON'T GET GREEDY.***
Expiry		***Trade Your Plan.***
Position Size		***TAKE PROFIT.*** ***Manage Risk.***
Total Premium		
Greeks		
Total Gain/Loss		
Successful?		

THINGS TO NOTE

TRADE PLAN

Date of Study	Type of Trade ☐ Swing Trading ☐ Day Trading ◯ Short ◯ Long
Asset Ticker	
Strategy	

	Target Entry	Target Exit
Asset Price		
Call/Put		
Premium		

LIVE TRADE

TRADE YOUR PLAN AND PLAN YOUR TRADES.
NO EMOTIONS ALLOWED.

	Actual Entry	Actual Exit
Date/Time		
Strike		***DON'T GET GREEDY.*** *Trade Your Plan.* ***TAKE PROFIT.*** *Manage Risk.*
Expiry		
Position Size		
Total Premium		
Greeks		
Total Gain/Loss		
Successful?		

THINGS TO NOTE

TRADE PLAN

Date of Study	Type of Trade ☐ Swing Trading ☐ Day Trading ◯ Short ◯ Long

Asset Ticker	

Strategy

	Target Entry	Target Exit
Asset Price		
Call/Put		
Premium		

LIVE TRADE

TRADE YOUR PLAN AND PLAN YOUR TRADES.
NO EMOTIONS ALLOWED.

	Actual Entry	Actual Exit
Date/Time		
Strike		***DON'T GET GREEDY. Trade Your Plan. TAKE PROFIT. Manage Risk.***
Expiry		
Position Size		
Total Premium		
Greeks		
Total Gain/Loss		

Successful?

LESSONS LEARNED

This is a space to take note of any new indicators you've learned and lessons from mistakes you've made from these last 5 trades.

Beginner and Advanced Options Trading Courses at Dreamfarmer.org

What is an Option?

The Right to Buy or Sell Something at a Specific Price

CALL= Right to Buy

If Price ↑ Gain Profit $ $ $

If Price ↓ Premium Paid is Loss $

PUT= Right to Sell

If Price ↑ Premium Paid is Loss $

If Price ↓ Gain Profit $ $ $

1 Contract = 100 Shares

Options Used On

What's The Trend?

Bullish ↑ — Price @ Support?
- YES → BUY
- NO → DON'T TRADE

Sideways — Wait For Breakout

Bearish ↓ — Price @ Resistance?
- YES → SELL
- NO → DON'T TRADE

Made in United States
Troutdale, OR
11/03/2026

56853160R00071